SMALL POINTED THINGS

Erica McAlpine is Associate Professor of English at Oxford and the A.C. Cooper Fellow in English at St Edmund Hall. Her book *The Poet's Mistake* appeared from Princeton University Press in 2020; a collection of poems, *The Country Gambler*, was published by Shearsman in 2016.

SMALL
POINTED
THINGS

ERICA McALPINE

CARCANET POETRY

First published in Great Britain in 2025 by
Carcanet
Main Library, The University of Manchester
Oxford Road, Manchester, M13 9PP
www.carcanet.co.uk

Text copyright © Erica McAlpine 2025

The right of Erica McAlpine to be identified as the author
of this work has been asserted in accordance with the
Copyright, Design and Patents Act of 1988; all rights reserved.
No part of this book may be used or reproduced in any manner
for the purpose of training artificial intelligence technologies or systems.

A CIP catalogue record for this book is
available from the British Library.

ISBN 978 1 80017 477 1

Set in Caslon Pro and Albertus Monotype
Book design by Andrew Latimer, Carcanet
Typesetting by LiteBook Prepress Services
Printed in Great Britain by SRP Ltd, Exeter, Devon

The publisher acknowledges financial
assistance from Arts Council England.

CONTENTS

I

Bats and Swallows	13
La Farfalla / The Moth	15
Woman Waiting	16
My Life as a Manatee	17
Whole, Some	18
Carpenter Bee	20
Moths	21
Pumpkins and Swans	22
Clementines	23
Spirits	24
The Scorpion	26
Ladybirds	27

II

The Thing About Ideas	31
Theory	33
What Fires	34
The Second Warthogs	35
Los Angeles	36
Pickle	37
Lord Knows Your Ship	39
Boat Trip	40
After Math	41
Two Riddles	42
1. Letter of Regret	42
2. Words of Intent	42
Upon Being Asked	43
Hoops	44

III

The Fountain	47
The Hour of Long Shadows	48
Arethusa	50
Debonair	51
Needlefish	52
Bananas, Milk, Sugar, and Stir	53
Spider	54
Holding Up the Moon	55
Some Words Between Them	56
Separate Fields	57
You	58
Kingfishers	59

IV

Digging the Well	63
Sungold	65
Rain	66
Baucis and Philemon	68
Wishbone	71
The Return	73
Triolet On My Mother's 74th Birthday	75
Stirrings	76
Love-lies-bleeding	78
Bringing It Down	79
Snowdrops	81
Blackbirds	82

Acknowledgements	85

for Grant and May

SMALL POINTED THINGS

I

BATS AND SWALLOWS

Whatever the difference might be
to one who knows,
we couldn't see
from where we stood in soft shadows
any signs that they were swallows

or bats. That there were wings
was without doubt;
you could see small pointed things
swooping out
into the gloaming –

and sometimes back.
One seemed almost iridescent
as I tried to track
its crescent
flight across the hill. The lack

of sound suggested
bats to me;
you strained to see if they nested
somewhere below the
terrace, having rested

your case on swallows.
We couldn't be sure
either way – and so it follows
that neither of us knows.
But since it is in your nature

always to side one way
or the other, you hold
that they were swallows. I say
the question never gets old,
that either, or both, hold sway.

LA FARFALLA / THE MOTH

after Petrarch

In August, out on the veranda, it
is not uncommon for a moth to fly
into the light and singe its wings to dust.
The lantern is so beautiful – it must.
I used to watch them burn and wonder why,
before I came to understand the bit
about desire, how there's no gentle landing,
not when it comes to fire. Your eyes demanding
mine, I'd fly into them every time
despite my certain harm and your regret.
You look away, and still, I seek them out.
Hellbent on serving my affliction, I'm
less bothered by my own pain than your doubt.
Although I burn, I haven't perished yet.

WOMAN WAITING

You have seen her in paintings gazing
out the window with its curtains
slightly parted, or staring, uncertain,
down a tangled lane, or in churches, silently phrasing
wishes for something amazing.

Her waiting could also be mundane,
like growing her hair long,
or listening to the radio for a favourite song,
or sitting on a plane.
She might have gone insane

waiting for what never came,
except that staying unsure
about waiting's cure
has always been part of waiting's game.
But what if she had had no aim?

Now there's something I could aspire
to – waiting just for the sake of
it. What would you make of
my being bent on nothing prior
and content without a trace of desire?

Waiting would be what I'd do
were it possible to cope,
having severed patience from hope.
You would try to
find me where I waited – not for you.

MY LIFE AS A MANATEE

Yes, I would be huge.
But it wouldn't trouble
my vanity,
for I'd have left humanity
behind. Seeking quiet refuge
in a bubble

on the morning of my change,
suddenly I'd burst
through, with flippers.
It would be strange
at first –
beneath speedboats and clippers

I'd glide
peacefully, so big and
so vague. And you, on the land,
you could turn
manatee, too, if you tried.
Anyone can learn.

Just imagine floating loosely under
the jetty, propelled
ever-so-slightly
by your tail, utterly unsightly,
yet always beheld
with wonder.

WHOLE, SOME

Like a piece of lemon sole,
Aunt Clara was deboned.
A man had come, she owned,
scooped her up whole,

and pulled out every line
that held her straight.
We found her, as on a plate,
claiming she was fine,

still retaining her shape,
decorated with parsley.
We would scarcely
know she'd had a scrape

but for moving her –
then it was a case
of lifting all at once, at pace,
or else disproving her

form completely.
We got the feeling
she liked it some, this being freewheeling.
She would stay discreetly

this way, thank
you very much.
You can look, but don't touch.
Our hearts sank

to think of what he stole
from her and what she was forsaking.
But she was good at faking
being whole.

CARPENTER BEE

Sometimes a thing
comes out of the woodwork
with more hostility than grace.
You're supposed to hold still,
remain calm, stay in one place,

not run away and go berserk
or shield your face. Otherwise it will
think you're threatening
it when it is threatening
you. You're part of the sting.

MOTHS

It starts with a glint
of gold upon a single sweater.
Who didn't know better
would think it was only lint.

But soon the tell-tale fluttering of buff
around your closet
and a thin deposit
on the shelves of something rough,

until across your woollens spread
those ghostly sleeves
the larvae leave
as they devour, thread

by thread, the handiwork
of a hundred knitters' hours.
Things are no longer in your power
to fix. More eggs lurk,

always, always – you're beaten
by an army of wings tiny
fringed and shiny.
Everything's half-eaten,

and getting ready
in the morning means being surrounded,
no, confounded,
by gold confetti.

PUMPKINS AND SWANS

Remember Eddie's story
about swans
landing in his pumpkin fields?
So much white
unexpected glory
scurrying over a season's
leftover yields.
They surely had their reasons
for wanting those bright
orbs – weighed the pros and cons
of stopping mid-flight.
But the image
of their ghostly plumage
haunting such large orange balls
still appals.
Something wasn't right.

CLEMENTINES

New Year's Day – another turning
of the sphere, with all we planned
in yesteryear as close to hand
as last night's coals left unmanned
in the fire, still orange and burning.

It is the season for clementines
and citrus from Seville
and whatever brightness carries us until
leaves and petals once more fill
the treetops and the vines.

If ever you were to confess
some cold truth about love's
dwindling, now would be the time – less
in order for things to improve
than for the half-bitter happiness

of peeling rinds
during mid-winter
recalling days that are behind
us and doors we cannot re-enter
and other doors we couldn't find.

SPIRITS

Sometimes we would rather court
the implausible than admit
how fallible we are.

I remember it –
how we both denied any part
in almost setting the house on fire.

It must have been a poltergeist
who got the peaches balanced in a bowl
suddenly to twitch

and roll
halfway across the counter, coming to rest
exactly on the switch

of the electric kettle.
We were lucky you smelled
the burn –

water boiled
dry against the metal –
in time to turn

it off. You denied leaving
a peach anywhere near it,
nor could I have –

neither of us would hear it.
So you settled on believing
some unholy spirit gave

orders from a nook or cranny
in our kitchen shelves.
I can see it

for what it was, whereas you think the uncanny
lives outside ourselves –
in ghosts. That must be it.

THE SCORPION

Top-heavy and front-loaded,
he barges into the ring, moving
as though he were shoving
or being goaded,

a prizefighting champion
posing and preposterous
and plated like a tiny rhinoceros
pitted against the giant Orion.

Exposing him gets his back
up. He'd have us quail
at his forward-curling tail
and be wary of cracks

in rocks and cleaving bark
where, venomous, crepuscular,
he hides with arms comically muscular
and a dozen eyes for sensing dark.

One glimpse of his carapace
will shock us –
brandishing pincers like maracas –
and his sting, the coup de grâce!

LADYBIRDS

A ladybird, or ladybug (call it
what you will) has crept
onto my pillowcase –
this one so small it
can hardly be seen. Except
I *do* see it; it is marking the place
where I slept

like a bloodstain.
You shrug, tell me it's good luck,
give our duvet a perfunctory sweep.
But I cannot possibly sleep
here: on the windowpane
a new brood crawls and keeps
watch – we are sitting ducks.

It happens almost every night:
cloaked in red,
one marauder, or two, takes flight,
infiltrates our bed
with dishevelled wings – something thin and black
always trailing sideways from its back,
which it eventually pulls tight

as if tucking its own covers
in. Semi-annual, this infestation
nevertheless surprises us, like the changing of the clocks.
The first few we discover
have the charm of snowflakes
(no two the same!), but soon a whole nation
of scarlet flocks

to the house: a British
invasion. Once adored
but now *persona-non-grata*:
isn't it always the way? Two on the headboard
are making me skittish –
one in bloodred, poured
with black, the other flecked terracotta.

II

THE THING ABOUT IDEAS

'No ideas but in things'

Someone put the beans on!
The end of the day has arrived;
the end of a very long summer. We survived.
Time to put jeans on.

Time to heat the tortillas.
Time to make the guacamole.
No intellectual rigmarole
here – the thing about ideas

isn't that you can't do much
with them, but that you can bend
them every which way to no end.
There's nothing to touch

in ideas. You can't eat them.
Someone please take out the chicken!
Ideas interest but don't make the heart quicken
like bodies do. You can't heat them

like sauce. They can be elliptical
in the worst way,
or too convoluted even to say.
I am sceptical

of a sustained interest in
ideas. Philosophers aren't,
but I am. You can't parent
or get dressed in

ideas like you can in cashmere.
Can someone please set the table!
Things rarely cause as much trouble
as ideas do. Middle-of-the-night fears

are made of ideas morning
disproves. You can sidestep a thing that you
see coming, but ideas come at you
without warning,

nor will they placate
your children. *Finish the cheese*
in your bowl, please –
and pick up your plate

and bring it to the sink.
It's late – no more time for playing
today. *Listen to what I'm saying!*
No time to think.

THEORY

*'all there is at the end is theory, art having finally become
vaporized in a dazzle of pure thought about itself'*
— Arthur Danto

What is poetry
but a dazzle
of pure thought
about itself? All
poems are inward-
facing. Even
the poetry of praise
could be called
navel-gazing.
Is it self-love
or just a method
for embracing
the endless potential
for turning
self-referential?
Poetry's thinking
draws a cavity
by its own gravity –
like something sinking
in. And as for
being pure,
nothing less sure
of itself could
dazzle more.

WHAT FIRES

Bougainvillea,
still trumpeting,
why do you hide
three burnt-out matchsticks inside?

What fires, long
past being fanned,
do you tuck away, conceal
all evidence of?

Lantern of spring,
flower of an idea,
papery past thirst, pink beyond real,

would it be so wrong
to burn, heal, and
still harbour love?

THE SECOND WARTHOGS

I saw them from the canal, nosing
their way through a spare enclosure behind
the zoo. Dusk-grey, two-of-a-kind,
and utterly unimposing,

they were traipsing aimlessly
across their corner of Regent's Park
like a pair of sullen cast-offs from the Ark
and wearing their dirt shamelessly.

Who could blame them for their ennui?
They were just the second
warthogs, their features having been reckoned
by some zookeeper as not-quite-worthy

of being seen. Oh to be prima ballerinas!
Not just understudies
sent back to paddocks muddied
by packs of hyenas

but actual queens!
Believe me when I say there was nothing shoddy
about them. They were half head, half body,
and their tusks were terribly clean.

LOS ANGELES

The life we could have had!
We'd have bought
a house, I should have thought –
angular, timber-clad,

dotted with cactuses
in a modern courtyard
for growing radishes and chard.
And our friends, famous actresses,

would always note
how tasteful
it was – nothing wasteful,
yet so lush! We'd serve entrecote,

brownies with sea salt,
grilled zucchini with lemon,
do whatever you do when
you're living on a fault

but not thinking about it –
grow agave, cover everything in sisal,
enjoy what is paradisal
without stopping to doubt it.

PICKLE

When you're lost for time, up late again,
too busy working to recognize
the depth and the size
of the problem, when there's no plan,

no solution save
for giving up and starting over
at square one, like a forsaken lover,
when the weather misbehaves

and spoils your fruits before you eat them,
and your luck has changed
so that everything must be rearranged,
and the odds are so bad you can't beat them,

you're in a pickle.
The situation has both soured
and preserved, and you're overpowered
by what began as a trickle

but grew into a torrent.
This isn't what you deserved,
but the pickle has been served
up neat, abhorrent,

like running into a brick wall.
You realise there is no cure
like vinegar
and salt, how fickle

life is, how far
you can be led before
finding out what's in store
for you is a lidded jar.

LORD KNOWS YOUR SHIP

Lord knows your ship
of sadness doesn't so much stop
as search for other ports. The trip
is usually short –
less a journey than a hop

back to some old familiar spot
where it can stay
awhile, trying not
to float away, or lying
low, to keep itself at bay.

BOAT TRIP

The point of no return
is always sooner than you think.
Rarely is there a sign.
The moment you discover
you want to go
back, you have crossed
the invisible line –
the port is way, way
behind you, the world is spinning,
and you are seasick
and in trouble:
to recover
the distance you've gone
would almost double
the length of the ride.
You didn't burn
any bridges – this is the Mediterranean
and there is no 'other side' –
but you're closer to the brink
than the beginning.
The trick
would have been to know,
way back in the bay,
that the sea was tempest-tossed.

AFTER MATH

> *'The number 3 does not occur in the past of the number 5'*
> *— Adam Frank*

Yet what happens has consequences.
This always leads to *that*.
Fiddle with the thermostat,
you get hot. Talk also incenses –

though not right away.
What gets said grows
a little – fans and blows,
bit by bit, day by day,

until there's a fire on your hands.
You never learn
how it started because everybody burns
to a crisp. Plots are planned,

fates are sealed,
everything is perfected
by strands that are connected
as meaning is concealed,

and you move from next
to next without fully knowing
the direction you're going.
And there is always a subtext.

So you had better
pay attention
to everything that gets a mention,
right down to the letter.

TWO RIDDLES

1. Letter of Regret

Without me, you
were a tall white bird.
You say you preferred
that bird to

what you became –
that you are no better
for receiving my letter
and wish you'd stayed the same.

2. Words of Intent

When we
live apart, you're dry and warm
and turn into another form
of me.

But together we
have prior
purpose and deep desire
and are meant to be.

UPON BEING ASKED

What you want is to say *no*
but have it sound like you said *yes*.
How is anybody's guess.
One word isn't two.
Sometimes *no thank you*
comes close – but only if pitched like you're
doing them a favour
by saying so,
as if you should
and really must answer *no*,
but do so unwillingly, as though
the offer were really good.

HOOPS

These hoops!
I am too big to jump through
them – my hips bump into
the sides and *oops*

they've clattered down
like fences do in storms.
Stop sending me forms
to fill that don't matter. I won't be shown

where to sign
or feel forced to report
the details of my falling short.
I'll doodle on the dotted line

dreaming of bars
low enough to step over
and laughing at the giver
of gold stars.

III

THE FOUNTAIN

Was I a goddess, or grotesque?
My tiny baby dozed
in her bassinet, and secretly I posed,
postpartum, statuesque,

underneath our double rain shower
wet with steam and spray
but more grateful than I could say
to have this respite of an hour.

I was nothing like Diana
bathing in the wood
as poor, stunned Acteon stood
watching her in awe –

more like Arethusa, who
herself became the fountain.
My chest grew into mountains,
and from their peaks two

pure white streams were sprouting,
spraying with the force
of some half-forgotten source
within me shouting

to get out. I warmed
to this new self of mine
and wondered if I'd turned divine
or been transformed.

THE HOUR OF LONG SHADOWS

It was the hour of long shadows.
Because you were brave, I thought
to teach you a little – as any mother ought
who wishes her daughter to know

something of the dark that lurks
within plain sight. 'See the shape
following you? You cannot escape
it – stepping sideways won't work,

it will always be right
there, even when you turn.'
I said it kindly, so you could learn,
but you didn't take it as you might.

Behind you, your shadow froze;
you swivelled round and took off running
with a three-year-old's cunning
before I could stop you. You chose

to run *at* it, but were vexed
when it jolted out in front of you
and bolted, always two
paces ahead. For what happened next,

neither of us was prepared.
As I hurried to catch you up from behind,
my own shade and yours combined
before you saw me, and you were scared.

The sun stretched before you the long
shadow of your pursuer.
Just your mother, not some evildoer –
but your face looked up to prove me wrong.

ARETHUSA

after Ovid

The waters fell silent as Arethusa rose
from the deep green within them.
She dried her hands in her drying hair.
And then she told how once, scouring
the woods, placing nets, she found
a stream whose soundless waters ran
seemingly without current, whose rocks
through clear depths shone to poplars
drinking and willows spreading silver
shade upon its banks. Weary and hot,
the goddess stopped to dip her feet
and then her knees until at last
she draped her clothing from a tree
and splashed full naked into the water.
The current was dragging from her hair.
But then she heard a voice rise up
around her – so she leapt onto the bank
to flee, and the river followed, filling
meadows and slopes with fast-moving water,
climbing rocks and bluffs, pressing forth
even when there was no way...
And the sun spread itself full across
her back, stretching tall before her
the shadow of her pursuer, and she
was circled by a cloud of mist, and
everywhere she stepped the waters pooled,
receiving from above the fountain
just now pouring from her hair.

DEBONAIR

The child saw something in the grass
no thicker than a piece of glass
or wider than a paper clip.
He picked it up – its mass

was like a chocolate chip.
Old clay pipe! Or just the tip
off of a broken one, he thought.
He brought it to his lips

although he knew that he should not.
Pretending it was hot,
he puffed and gave his chin a stroke,
and as he played he half forgot

himself within his private joke.
And then a thought within him woke –
that no one else should see him smoke.
He slipped the pipe into his cloak.

NEEDLEFISH

In that instant,
dear daughter,
when they flashed
like cupid's arrow

through the current
of saltwater
where you splashed,
more narrow

and more terse
than any gleam,
I thought I felt
within my gut

love's old curse
entering the dream –
that through no fault
of yours but

beauty, fresh
as it is fierce,
you should become
as bait

to any fish
whose point would pierce,
as if from
nowhere, while I wait.

BANANAS, MILK, SUGAR, AND STIR

When your mother-cup's a sieve
no amount of sleep can fill, try this: a bowl,
one banana (peeled), a glass of whole
milk, a tablespoon (give

or take) of sugar, and a stick for stirring.
Cut up the banana in halved slices,
sprinkle generously with sugar (this entices
the children), stop worrying

about nutritional value (you are absolved
by the banana), and pour in the milk.
Twirl it with the stick until it's like silk
and the sugar has dissolved.

Serve.

SPIDER

gangewifre (Old English): a weaver as she goes

She who weaves as she goes along
has left behind her silks in nooks
and up in lofts and piles of books
as if to shuttle them were wrong.

I find them wound around the stair,
and tucked in corners of the ceiling
where I brush them down – this feeling
like combing through a baby's hair.

If she could take me for a spin,
I'd know the softness of her cords
and learn the ropes of how they're stored
within her spooling abdomen.

Forever she is disentangling
self from string; she seems to hold no
stake in anything she sews.
She weaves and leaves it dangling,

whose home is neither made for long
nor wanting in its strength of spoke,
who cares for delicacy of stroke
but draws the singer from the song.

HOLDING UP THE MOON

She held it perilously
up, with cupped hands,
on tip-toe,
while her brother querulously
made demands
that soon
it would be his turn to have a go
holding up the moon.

But it was too late
for him.
The moon went dim
as it rose through a cloud
as if to declare
that heaven isn't fair
and only some are allowed
celestial state.

Later, higher,
the moon went bright
again. I was alone,
and cold,
and full of desire,
and it was too far gone
into the night
to hold.

SOME WORDS BETWEEN THEM

Two spheres on meeting may so softly collide
They stay, as if still kissing, side by side.
— *Walter de la Mare*

I heard, I swore, some words between them,
the dangling moon to the dawn
one silent pink morning upon
the uncertain hour. Her blushing warmth went sallying
forth to the slow moon's dilly-dallying,
and there I saw a knowing glance:
one peered up, the other down, by chance.

I think they thought no one had seen them,
their light commingling of realms
in a lilac sky behind silhouetted elms –
it was her fingers reaching up for the moon's toes
where the heavens turned bright.
And the moon calling 'Good night, Morning' in the rose,
and the dawn's 'Good morning, Night.'

SEPARATE FIELDS

Sometimes we walk
down the hill
on different tracks.
We don't have to talk.
You will always check
for sheep stuck
on their backs.
I am in *Christina's World*.
She is lying still
not-quite-centred
in the field.
I don't think she
noticed
when I entered
this remotest
of places
where I cannot see
either of your faces.

YOU

The lamb
was breach,
but you
knew
what to do.
You
reached
your hand,
ungloved,
into the ewe,
shoved
the lamb
back, and
then
pulled through
one leg, two,
and then
the head.
And when
you said
it wasn't dead,
oh phew
I said,
oh phew.

KINGFISHERS

I am no connoisseur
of kingfishers,
but one flew
past me with its blue
metallic armour

as I crossed
a railroad track.
I only glimpsed its back –
freckled, glossed
with black –

before it dove into
a hedge and through.
How absurd
for this bird
to have anything to do

with trains,
who lives
on fish, not grains,
and shares a habitat with cranes
and egrets. But life gives

itself over
purely to whatever
is near it.
And then I could hear it,
a river.

IV

DIGGING THE WELL

On our plot between the river
and the railroad track,
there is a well. We discovered
it by chance – weeds had covered
all but a sliver
of its rim,
which time had filled to the brim
with soil and rock.

Was the earth calling,
like something long asleep,
to be heaved up
from the deep
where her stolen daughter
sets a table of water
for filling buttercups?
Ignoring the risk of falling

in, we dug as far as we could go
with our digging hoe.
And then we sent our son down.
Up he looked at us and laughed –
oblivious as a canary in the shaft.
He couldn't drown;
it was mid-July
and the well was dry.

But there we saw
in that short space
between us and his little face
the length of life's string –
and felt the sting
of knowing we draw
from our own grave
to water what we have.

SUNGOLD

Her favourite tomato was sungold –
I know because I remember,
one late August or early September,
being together, and being told

to marry them with bread, basil, mozzarella,
a little olive oil, just a pinch of salt.
It was too good – to a fault.
I will never again eat panzanella

or pick sungolds off the vine
without thinking of how her life would stop
so soon after that bumper crop,
when everything was fine.

RAIN

Occasionally you can sense
what's strange
about something so mundane
as relentless November rain.
You tense
up at the same old change

in atmosphere,
the blue sky
moving from clear
to muddled.
How it must have befuddled
those who didn't know why,

who were the very first
to contend
with so much water
falling from so high, fearing the worst.
Who would send
such floods but to slaughter

or smother?
It would be inconceivable
to think so big a downpour
could be anything other
than war.
Unbelievable

how we've
still not put a stop to it —
found a reprieve
for rain. We live through it
like we were always okay
with being washed away.

BAUCIS AND PHILEMON

after Ovid

In Phrygia, among the watery hills,
a lime tree grows beside an oak. There is
no limit to the power of the gods.
For here it was, upon this very spot,
that Jupiter and Mercury, disguised
as men, descended to a little town,
and seeking out some shelter there among
a thousand homes, and finding none, approached
at last the humblest roof – a cottage thatched
from straw. In this place, sweet old Baucis and
her Philemon were married and grown old,
had lived their lives contented, although poor,
and spent each happy day together free
from care. So when the gods arrived there, dressed
as strangers, lowering through their lowly door,
the old man set up stools, and Baucis stirred
a flame within their hearth from day-old coals
and even added kindling from their roof.
She picked and peeled a cabbage from the garden
while Philemon carefully pierced with a pronged stick
the pork that he had hung up many weeks
before from blackened beams; then, trimming off
a piece of that prized meat, he laid it on
the fire for it to cook. And all the while
their talking stole the best part of an hour,
so they draped blankets on their willow bench,
and Jupiter and Mercury reclined
as Baucis – even with her trembling hands –
levelled the wobbly table with the lid
of an old pot and wiped it clean with two

fresh sprigs of mint. And then she dressed it full
of plump, green olives, cornel cherries soaked
in lees of wine, endives and radishes,
sweet home-made creams and cheeses, hens' eggs cooked
upon the turning ashes – and all of this
in earthen dishes, hand-carved beechwood cups
all lined with wax inside, from which the wine
soon drained as steaming plates came to replace
the last – here nuts and figs and sedge, here plums
and sweetest smelling apples, grapes just-picked
from twisting vines, a jar of glistening honey –
until old Philemon, noticing how
the bowls seemed to refill themselves, and how
new wine was welling up in finished jugs,
abruptly threw his body down in prayer
to thank these gods just now betraying themselves,
and tried to offer them his only goose.
The goose went flapping up – would not be caught –
when Jupiter exclaimed, 'My goodly man,
preserve your goose! Come follow us into
these mountains: we will flood the homes of all
your wicked neighbours but shall spare you both!'
And while the gods revenged themselves upon
the villagers, poor Baucis wept. But then
she saw her tiny cottage rise into
a temple – marble columns springing from its
forked supports – and all the rustic thatch
was turning into gold as two broad gates
were swinging wide above the polished floors.
Jupiter spoke once more: 'Now tell us what
you wish for, dear man, with his honest wife.'
And after some quick words with Baucis, he
quietly said: 'We ask only to serve
as guardians of your shrine, and since we've lived

all our lives blessed with happiness, to have
the self-same hour bear us both away,
that I should never see Baucis's grave
nor she see mine.' And that was how it happened:
they cared for and protected that temple
for the rest of their days, until old age
had so weakened their frail bodies that
they stood holding each other at the shrine
whispering stories of their life together.
Then poor, elderly Baucis saw that her
dear Philemon was growing leaves, which she
soon too began to grow. And as the bark
rose up enveloping their wrinkled faces,
together to each other they both cried,
'Farewell, my love!' And at that very moment,
they were subsumed at the exact same time.
Anyone can visit these trees, their trunks
forever intertwined. I have been there
and seen them for myself. Who care for gods
become as gods – who honour them are honoured.

WISHBONE

Falling asleep tonight,
I remember your tree –
mature now, standing at a great height,
but years before you met me
a chestnut held tight

in your palm.
Was it your pride this evening over some
small thing that made me think
of it, here at the brink,
when the world turns briefly calm

and the children are asleep
in their rooms?
Once, in order to keep
it growing straight as a broom,
you had to replant it deep,

removing a limb where it split
near the base,
digging it
up at the roots, rejigging it
into place

like an arrow,
not a wishbone.
You love the straight and narrow.
I'm the one
of the two of us more prone

to changes in direction
and bending about,
a trait you regard mostly with affection,
or beyond correction,
since some things can't be straightened out.

THE RETURN

'fies nobilium tu quoque fontium'

– Horace, Odes 3.13

We drove our rental car from Rome
to somewhere I had been before.
I didn't have to twist your arm
to come – your patience with me wore
the dress of love's first tenderness –
and though the famous spring I'd missed
the first-time round might not exist,
together we would try and guess
the spot and see what we could find.
It was too hot – for all except
ourselves and one old man who slept
inside his car (we parked behind
him, passing as we climbed). The spring
was no more hidden than a thing
placed in your palm as if to shame
the person who would make a game
of looking for it. Much like glass
it shone – 'brighter than glass' Horace
had said – though not 'bedecked with flowers.'
(This small discrepancy was ours
to note.) Its basins towered like
a giant three-tiered wedding cake
with crystal-clear ganache. We dipped
our hands in – cold. Something skipped
across the surface of the water.
We had disturbed the pond skaters.

'Well, this is it,' I said – and you
agreed. With nothing else to do,
we turned around; but heading down,
we saw the old man climbing up.
He waved at us as if he'd known
us all our lives, then filled his cup
with water from the spring, and drank.

TRIOLET ON MY MOTHER'S 74TH BIRTHDAY

You cannot imagine one season in another.
A warm body doesn't remember the cold
or see, in its dazzled eyes, anything other.
You cannot imagine one season in another.
You cannot imagine life without your mother.
These present gifts, so green and gold –
you cannot imagine one season in another.
A warm body doesn't remember the cold.

STIRRINGS

Something stirred while I was tulip cutting.
It wasn't wind – no wind was there.
It wasn't Gus the terrier
along his rounds of garden strutting.

It couldn't be a beast of air –
the rustle I had heard
wherever it occurred
had come from somewhere

down among the rows
of new potatoes. Had I seen white
in my peripheral sight?
A rabbit's tail or nose?

No, nothing so simple
as rabbits. Rabbits live in burrows;
here were only furrows
and dimples.

Hares! Three leverets asleep
in a warm round
heap. I scanned the ground
for their mother. Would she keep

her distance, let them
be alone with me? Would she stay calm
or circle round us like a helicopter mom?
Or forget them,

being hare-brained?
Surely somewhere, ears erect,
she stood sentry to protect,
her amber eyes trained

on me. She would not know, or care,
that I was someone's mother –
I was only other,
neither her, nor hare.

LOVE-LIES-BLEEDING

Greeks called it amaranth, 'unfading,'
seeing how its flowers keep
their colour even as they weep.
But to watch its slow cascading

brings a certain kind of shame:
surely some wounded lover
hung low by love's being over
lies behind its English name.

Look and be horror-stricken:
furry tentacles unspool
and gather in pink pools,
red ropes elongate and thicken,

grow nearly to a finger's girth.
You might be strangled
by them quickly if entangled
and bound forever to the earth.

Cut and droop them from high vessels.
Let such frightening inflorescence
dangle for you in essence –
become no more than tassels.

BRINGING IT DOWN

It took three men
half a day to do it –
to bring down
almost before we knew it
our sixty-foot cedar.
Calk-booted Jack,
more monkey than man,
and Ross, back-
and-forth to the chipper,
and Merlin, with the plan,
something like their leader.
Branches first,
some as thick as birches,
stripped and thrown
and landing with a thump.
It looked demanding
but within hours only the trunk
was left standing
with nothing on top,
bare as a match,
or a finished
lollipop.
To be so diminished!
But trees don't have hopes
like we do. Only doves
will wonder where it got to,
and squirrels flinging
limb to limb above
the stump. Log

by log, lump
by lump, Ross
carried away what
Jack cut
while swinging,
king of ropes.

SNOWDROPS

What if this virgin-
coloured cluster
huddled close against
the cold and bluster
were all the hue a spring-time
field could muster?

Accustomed
to such deprivations,
would we crave
the lichen's grey and white striations,
or knots of black on birches,
like dalmatians,

or stuff that blows
in gales across the rough,
like hail – the pussy
willow's silver fluff?
Would black-and-whiteness
be enough?

BLACKBIRDS

'She is brown,'
I said to you,
less in annoyance
than wonder
when she flew
past us with a certain flamboyance
not over but under
our gate
to settle down
into the tree beside her mate.

'But he is black,'
you replied,
'and the name is his.'
'As it always is,'
I poked.
'I was your bride
and took your name,
yet we are not the same.'
You'd have joked
back

but couldn't deny it.
We grew quiet
when we heard the blackbirds
sharing words
between them.
Whose song
it was we would
never know, not having seen them
sing. But it would be wrong
to say, even if we could.

ACKNOWLEDGEMENTS

Thank you to the editors of the following magazines, where several of these poems first appeared:

The American Scholar: 'Love-lies-bleeding', 'Spider', 'The Hour of Long Shadows', 'The Thing About Ideas', and 'Woman Waiting'

The Atlantic: 'Bats and Swallows'

Bad Lilies: 'Snowdrops'

Liberties: 'Blackbirds', 'Ladybirds', 'La Farfalla/The Moth' and 'Needlefish'

The New Criterion: 'Carpenter Bee' and 'Whole, Some'

The New Statesman: 'Hoops'

The New York Review of Books: 'The Second Warthogs'

The Times Literary Supplement: 'Two Riddles'

'Some Words Between Them' was commissioned by Angela Leighton for *Walter de la Mare: Critical Appraisals* (Liverpool: Liverpool University Press, 2022)